MW00774951

What People / Have Your Heart's Desire
Tools for a Wealthier, Healthier, Happier Life

"What a jewel of a book this is! And how WONDERFUL to have Mr. Irion's wisdom brought back into manifestation in this way! This little volume will be SUCH a gift to the world!"

Peggy Day
Co-author,
Psychic Children: A Sign of Our Expanding Awareness

"Author Carol Chapman delivers an up-beat hopeful message that we can change our lives in many ways and describes why and how to do so. As the first installment of *Your Spiritual Awakening* series, the author gives practical examples of using tools such as gratitude lists and specific prayers for manifestation, forgiveness, and release of resentment with guidelines on the wording and time frame for the greatest results. Furthermore, many examples are shared with the reader to show the varied results and the impact that the prayers had as well as how J. Everett Irion helped guide and lead Carol at a young age to use the power of prayer."

Lindy van Burik
Co-moderator, the Edgar Cayce Forum
Virginia Beach, VA, USA

"This little book allowed me to reach a deeper appreciation of all that life offers; to see the perfection of my life's path; and from that place, a more humble heart emerged as I followed Carol's prescribed route to manifesting my heart's desires through the auspices of prayer."

Shannon Wills
Nanaimo, BC, Canada

Your Spiritual Awakening

HAVE YOUR

HEART'S

DESIRE

TOOLS FOR A WEALTHIER, HEALTHIER, HAPPIER LIFE

by

Carol Chapman

SunTopaz LLC
Light Overcomes
Foster, Virginia

Your Spiritual Awakening
Have Your Heart's Desire
Tools for a Wealthier, Healthier, Happier Life

Copyright © 2012 by Carol Chapman
All Rights Reserved

Published by
SunTopaz LLC
P.O. Box 123, Foster, VA 23056
www.SunTopaz.com

Publisher's Cataloging-in-Publication
(Provided by Quality Books, Inc.)

Chapman, Carol (Carol Anne)
   Have your heart's desire : tools for a wealthier,
healthier, happier life / by Carol Chapman.
   p. cm. -- (Your spiritual awakening)
   Includes bibliographical references and index.
   ISBN-13: 978-0-9754691-3-2
   ISBN-10: 0-9754691-3-4

   1. Irion, J. Everett--Teachings. 2. Cayce, Edgar,
1877-1945. Edgar Cayce readings. 3. Forgiveness.
4. Spiritualism.   I. Irion, J. Everett. II. Cayce,
Edgar, 1877-1945. III. Title. IV. Series: Your
spiritual awakening.

BF1045.I58C43 2012   133.9
                      QBI09-600152

Edited by Clair Balsley and C.A. Petrachenko
Cover design by Clair Balsley; cover photo by Carol Chapman
Photos of the author by David Seaver Photography

*This book is available at quantity discounts for bulk purchases. For
information, email publisher@SunTopaz.com.*

*To the Higher Power that lies within
each and every one of us.*

Contents

Your Spiritual Awakening Series

When people discover that I first met my husband in a dream they want to know, "How did you do that? Were you doing anything special to make that happen?"

Well, yes! Of course I was doing something special beforehand! I'd been living a life of unfolding intimacy with my soul. For years, I have integrated short routines into my everyday life that help me to live with my soul's guidance.

Naturally, the additional questions that follow are along the lines of, "How can I do the things you have done?" and "Can you teach me?"

Again, the answer is a resounding, "Yes!"

I can share with you what I have learned and what I have integrated into my life to help further my spiritual awakening. By including these practices in your life, you too can help open the path to your spiritual awakening.

Many people look for a personal spiritual life coach. However, it turns out we all have one. It is with us all the time. It cares for us more deeply and more personally than any person could—even more than our mothers and fathers. It is our soul.

The fantastic thing is that your soul, which you can access through your subconscious, is connected with and is part of the Divine. Through your soul you can get spiritual guidance from the Creator. You can derive the benefits of living within spiritual laws, receive spiritual guidance, and receive the love and Grace that is your birthright. In addition, the more you open yourself to following your soul and to working *with* your soul, the more your soul makes itself available to you.

You may not know it, but you are already expressing your soul in the physical. Some of these effects you may already be aware of, such as gut feelings and intuitive insights. In some cases, information in the *Your Spiritual Awakening* series will merely awaken you to spiritual experiences you take for granted or that you do not realize are manifestations of your soul.

In other cases, you will be given techniques that will help you to develop your spiritual or soul abilities. Some of the techniques will easily work with your own particular soul talents. Other suggestions will not be so easy. We all have different soul, spiritual, and psychic abilities and different ways of manifesting these talents in our lives and the lives of others.

Although my spiritual journey started in my early childhood when I fell down the stairs and heard and saw angels singing, much of the direction for that quest in my adult years came from Edgar Cayce's psychic readings and my participation in Edgar Cayce Search for God Study Groups.

I also had the good fortune of knowing and being guided by J. Everett Irion. I benefited immensely from using the various techniques he developed based on his understanding of the Cayce readings.

Furthermore, I have been keeping a dream journal for years and working with my dreams, not just in trying to understand them, but also in following through with advice given in the dreams. After all, dreams come from your subconscious and your soul connects with your conscious mind through your subconscious.

In addition, I went to a hypnotherapist to seek help in resolving my excessive weight gain after a late-in-life miscarriage. During those sessions, to both of our surprise, I was given additional direction for strengthening the connection with my soul and, thus, improving my spiritual awareness. Some of the suggestions included loving and honoring the nature kingdom.

If you are interested in reading more about my spiritual awakening, and the story that has sparked the interest of so many readers to want to know more, it can be found in my first book, *When We Were Gods: Insights on Atlantis, Past Lives, Angelic Beings of Light, and Spiritual Awakening*, which is the revised expanded version of *The Golden Ones: From Atlantis to a New World*.

As I mentioned earlier, much of my adult spiritual journey was aided by the Edgar Cayce readings. In a trance reading given for himself, Edgar Cayce inquired as to the source of his psychic abilities. He was told that there is often confusion in the minds of those seeking or studying his psychic readings in that they do not understand that:

"... psychic IS of the SOUL."

~ Edgar Cayce Reading 254-185

Cayce must have delivered these words so emphatic-
ally that his secretary was compelled to write "IS" and
"SOUL" in capital letters.

And so, since "psychic IS of the SOUL," the *Your
Spiritual Awakening* series of books deals with the manifestation of your soul in your life, thereby awakening your
spiritual and psychic soul powers.

Your subconscious, which is connected to your soul,
enables a way for your conscious mind to access your soul
and your psychic abilities. Your subconscious holds all of
your memories, both from this life and all other existences
you've had. Through its connection with your soul, your
subconscious is connected to the Divine and all the
knowledge and power inherent in the Divine.

In the course of the *Your Spiritual Awakening* series, I
will share with you steps you can take, techniques you can
use, and ways to live day to day that will help strengthen
that connection between your conscious self and your soul.
I will also share real-life examples where people have used
the described guidelines.

Although these books are being released as a series,
they need not be read in the order that they were released.
In addition, each book is written so that it can stand alone.
As a result, books in the series can be read in any order, or
you may choose to only read certain titles within the
series. That being said, take what resonates with you and
use it to blossom. Enrich your life and the world around
you.

Foreword

There is no denying it. Profound changes are occurring at an alarming rate on our planet every day; hour by hour, minute by minute, moment by moment. From the overwhelming earthquake and tsunami in Japan, to the very personal relationship issues we each face in our daily lives, these often traumatic experiences are forcing us to re-evaluate our perceptions of the world, how we choose to cope with these life-changing events, and for many of us, how we view the effects of prayer on our circumstances. Do we have control of our own destinies? Is it within our ability to improve seemingly hopeless relationships? Is there a higher power or energy that can help us to bring more balance and joy into our lives? People are searching for answers.

As if on cue, Carol Chapman's brief, but richly poignant, book has arrived on the scene, filled with pithy examples of how she and many others found hope and help through the amazing, spiritual tools developed by a man named Everett Irion. Based on the premise that there is both a higher Creative Power/God in the world, of which we are all a part, as well as Universal Laws that govern all life, including humanity, Mr. Irion created innovative methods of prayer that can assist us in tapping into that reservoir of higher energy. These are tools that truly work, when applied from the heart.

My first encounter with Everett Irion occurred on a rather humorous note while I was standing on a small foot bridge over a very shallow goldfish pond. It was in the early 1980's, during my career at Edgar Cayce's Association for Research and Enlightenment (Cayce is considered America's best documented psychic). One of my favorite spots for lunch there was the Meditation Garden. While standing on the small foot bridge, I was in a reflective mood and was gazing intently at the water and newly bloomed water lilies, when a man's voice startled me out of my reverie.

"I hope you're not planning to jump," the voice said with a slight Texas twang.

When I turned to see who had made the tongue-in-cheek remark, I was surprised to see a slightly built, older gentleman whom I'd never met, with a shock of grayish white hair and wearing a bolo tie. He laughed when I assured him that I didn't intend to jump because I wasn't a very strong swimmer. We introduced ourselves, and he said that he was taking a break from his desk work and simply enjoying the beautiful weather. Little did I realize the depth of that "desk work" with which Mr. Irion was involved at that time.

Over the years, I frequently would see Everett in the garden or on the walkways between buildings, and our interactions were always the same—relaxed, joking, and filled with an appreciation for our surroundings and one another. All I knew about Everett (as he liked to be called) was that he was a C.P.A. who had worked most of his life as an accounting manager or comptroller. He never gave more details about himself.

It wasn't until much later that I discovered the full extent of Everett's involvement and dedication to the study of metaphysics, spiritual growth, and the material contained in Cayce's psychic discourses. Everett not only facilitated a dedicated group focused on his in-depth study of the Book of Revelation, but he subsequently published a book of commentaries on Cayce's discourses on that material as well. Everett also tackled the highly complex subject of vibrations, exploring the power and effect of vibrations in the universe. But the segment of Everett's work that affected me the most, personally, was the two 40-Day healing prayers he devised, which he wrote about in *Venture Inward Magazine* in 1985.

I had occasion to try Everett's 40-Day Prayer of Forgiveness in my own life and was blown away by the astounding positive effect it had on a troubling relationship. I later applied the 40-Day Prayer of Manifestation (based on the Law of Attraction), and had outstanding results with that process also. After those profound experiences, I felt compelled to share the benefits of the prayers with as many people as possible and frequently suggested them over the years in my intuitive dream counseling work. I continue to recommend this 40-Day approach to my family, friends, and to clients in my Shamanic energy healing sessions who are struggling with these issues in their lives.

Carol has done a superlative job of bringing the application of Everett's healing processes clearly into context for readers. Her touching and very human stories let us know that we are not alone in our efforts to grow and evolve spiritually. Perhaps, most importantly, Ms. Chapman has shown us that some remarkable tools are ready and waiting for us to try for ourselves on the journey to divine wholeness. Thank you, Everett, for following your heart's desire — and thank you, Carol, for presenting this information in such a highly readable, accessible form.

Nancy C. Chrisbaum
Filmmaker, Intuitive Counselor, and Energy Practitioner
Alexandria, Virginia

CHAPTER ONE
A Kind and Psychic Counselor

"The most beautiful experience we can have is the mysterious ..."

~ *Albert Einstein*, Bite-Size Einstein

Years ago I used to visit a delightful elderly gentleman by the name of J. Everett Irion. He was full of wisdom and kindness. He used to give individual counseling sessions at Edgar Cayce's Association for Research and Enlightenment (A.R.E.) in Virginia Beach, Virginia.

Everett was a quiet but powerful force in the background of the organization that grew up around the wisdom that came through the world's best documented psychic, Edgar Cayce.

A certified public accountant by training, Everett came to the A.R.E. to become business manager and treasurer of the organization. He told me that he journeyed to the A.R.E. at the request of Edgar Cayce's son, Hugh Lynn Cayce, who was president of the organization at that time.

As it turned out, Everett did much more than just the accounting at the A.R.E. He also had a lively inquiring mind and a fascination with the information in Edgar Cayce's psychic readings. Not only did Everett enjoy delving into the depths of the information that surfaced in Cayce's self-induced hypnotic trances, but Everett also enjoyed sharing the information he learned in lectures, books, and through individual counseling sessions such as the ones I attended.

At the time, I did not know that many people had benefited from counseling sessions with Everett. Over the years, I have met many individuals whose lives were blessed through their association with this wonderful man who was deeply dedicated to the concepts in the Cayce readings.

Everett's Psychic Abilities

The Cayce readings say psychic is of the soul. They give specific techniques for creating a better interaction with the soul so as to develop psychic abilities.

I assume Everett applied these psychic development techniques in his life. Rumors circulated about his psychic abilities.

For example, a friend told me how he had brought Everett a particularly difficult dream to interpret. Even though the friend had consulted numerous dream symbol dictionaries and talked with many friends, the young man could not understand the dream. He knew the dream held great importance in his life because of the emotion he had felt upon awakening.

During his session with Everett, my friend opened his dream journal to the place he had previously marked and began reading the dream out loud to Everett.

Before the young man could finish reading the dream, Everett said, "This is related to a dream you had before."

The young man looked up in surprise. He hadn't talked to Everett before. How could Everett know about any previous dreams?

"May I?" asked Everett, as he reached for the young man's dream journal.

My friend handed the book to Everett who said to the young man, "You drew a picture about it."

Now the young man felt truly intrigued. He admitted that he liked to draw pictures to illustrate some of his dreams. How could Everett know about this? Everett continued to leaf through the dream journal. Finally the older man stopped at a page with a drawing on it.

"There," Everett said, "there it is—your drawing. Now read this dream out loud, and we'll see how they both explain each other."

The young man said that Everett was right. Once he read the other dream, both of the dreams made sense.

Background

Many of the ideas presented here began in Everett's office years ago and culminated in my personal journey of spiritual discovery. It was Everett who taught me the 40-Day Manifestation Prayer and the 40-Day Forgiveness Prayer. He also taught me how to make choices based on his understanding of the principles in Edgar Cayce's psychic readings. In addition, Everett worked with me on interpreting dreams.

At the time of my visits with Everett, he was in his late 70s. I did not know that he had suffered a heart attack at the young age of 52 and that this event induced his career change and move from Texas to the A.R.E. in Virginia Beach. In spite of his early-in-life heart attack, he passed away at the ripe old age of 86. I would imagine that a lifestyle change based on the suggestions in Cayce's health readings led to his recovery and subsequent long and fulfilling life.

Edgar Cayce gave over 14,000 trance readings at the request of individuals who wanted help with physical conditions, better relationships, and greater success in business. He could reveal a person's purpose in life based on astrological factors and past lives. My favorite readings are the ones on metaphysics, philosophy, and Atlantis.

Although Mr. Cayce passed away in 1945, his psychic readings are available for anyone to read at the A.R.E There you can find one of the best metaphysical libraries in the United States.

CHAPTER TWO
Appreciate Everything

"The grateful outreaching of your mind in thankful praise to the Supreme Power is a liberation or expenditure of force; it cannot fail to reach that to which it is addressed. And, as a result, God responds with an instantaneous movement toward you."

~ *Wallace D. Wattles,* The Science of Getting Rich

As I said earlier, Everett was full of wisdom and kindness. During the time I had the good fortune to visit him, I learned many wonderful things. We used to have great discussions on the meaning of life.

Everett taught me to be thankful for everything. At first blush, this suggestion sounds like a Gratitude List, like those suggested by Oprah and *The Secret* (the popular book and movie describing the Law of Attraction).

Gratitude List
Both Oprah and *The Secret* recommend that you make a daily list of all that you have to be thankful for. This is wonderful, especially when you feel discouraged. It helps you to see how much there is in your life to appreciate. In

addition, when those inevitable hurts and losses occur, you can remind yourself of all that you have.

The Gratitude List is a great way to get you out of the trash can when the lid is wedged shut. There is nothing like being grateful for all that you have as a way of blasting that trash can lid off of your depression or your helpless feelings.

According to Rhonda Byrne, author of *The Secret*, gratitude is the first step in the process of attracting the things, relationships, health, and happiness we all strive for. It is an important step in the process of the Law of Attraction.

When you are grateful, it sets powerful forces to work in your life. When you emphasize all that you have to be thankful for, you become a person that attracts more items, relationships, and opportunities for which to be thankful. It works on the principle of like attracts like.

If you are a person who mainly complains or feels sorry for yourself, you attract more reasons to complain or pity yourself. However, if you are thankful — and you will be as you keep a Gratitude List consistently — you will attract more reasons to be grateful.

To my surprise, I have discovered that people I would never have suspected of keeping a Gratitude List do so. For example, I recently spent a week at a writer's retreat with a girlfriend who is a murder mystery writer. I've known this woman for a number of years and always saw her as a pragmatic and conservative person rather than a person who is open to body/mind/spirit concepts.

However, after a couple of days, she must have felt comfortable enough with me to mention, as she said good-night and traipsed off to her bedroom, that she had made some wonderful progress on her writing and therefore already knew what she was going to put on her Gratitude List.

"What?" I asked. "You keep a Gratitude List?"

She told me how much it helped her to list those things she felt grateful for before she went to bed.

"You have no idea how much this has helped in my work and in my life."

"But," she added, "I limit it to only five things per night. Otherwise, you can wear yourself out with the list and stop doing it."

I thought that was good advice. I realized that I had probably stopped keeping a Gratitude List because I had been writing too long a list and had become discouraged because of the time it took me.

In discussions with my friend about her Gratitude List, I also realized that in the past I had only included items in my personal life for which I felt grateful. I don't know why, but it never occurred to me to list items from my work and business. I now try to look at the whole spectrum of my life for items to include on my Gratitude List.

Taking Gratitude to the Next Level

The Law of Attraction has been around much longer than *The Secret*. Everett knew it well. He taught me to take gratitude even further. He told me to be thankful for *everything*, even the things I did not like. In fact, he advised me to be *especially* thankful for the things that are as frightening as a rhinoceros fuming and getting ready to charge. In other words, for those items in your life that you fear, hate, and dread.

"There is a spiritual law in the Universe," he told me again. "Like attracts like."

If all you can do is wail and moan, then all you will get is something more to wail and moan about. However, as soon as you start being thankful for *everything,* the Universe will rush to find ways to give you more things to be thankful for.

"What?" you say, "Be thankful for the husband who beats me, for the mother that drinks, for this lousy job, for this unemployment, for this financial disaster, for this handicap? You've got to be kidding. If I'm going to be thankful for all this, I'm just going to get more of the same."

No, Everett was not kidding. To begin, he did not mean that you should not feel angry for the troubles in your life. He did not mean to be passive or to be a doormat. Your anger helps you to figure out how to protect yourself and the ones you love. Everett did not mean you should be complacent for your lousy job or your alcoholic mother.

He did mean, though, that instead of spending your time feeling sorry for yourself or complaining, that if you felt grateful, you might see these difficulties as challenges instead of setbacks. You might see your problems as learning opportunities rather than disasters. In short, you might find the inner strength to better deal with your situation.

I suspect that Everett gave this advice to me because, at the time, I was going through a very difficult period in my first marriage. It was ending, and I was devastated. No, I was not handling the situation very well. I had bouts of rage and spent my time complaining, blaming, and feeling sorry for myself. Everett's advice: to be thankful for every-thing—"and, I mean *everything*"—was the best advice anyone ever gave me. It helped to stem my tendency to make things worse by wallowing in self pity and feeling helpless.

Everett was trying to get through to me that the all-powerful subconscious operates on different rules than the conscious mind. To many it may appear that a person can control their life by fighting against the difficulties that come up. However, in matters under the control of the subconscious, you make better headway by being thankful for those very circumstances in your life that appear to cause you the most distress.

"Why?" you may ask.

In J. Everett Irion's book, *Why Do We Dream?*, he explains that our souls have a greater idea of life than our conscious mind's limited understanding of our intended purpose. By giving thanks for everything, we show our faith in our Higher Nature and its purposes for us.

In *Why Do We Dream?*, Everett also explains:

"This understanding, if accepted rather than rejected, will come as a natural result of the operation of the living creative forces, as they bring us a quality of being that may well be incompre-hensible to our conscious minds, because it is imprinted in that first creation, which we cannot remember—This type of faith is inherent in a planted seed bringing forth fruit—By adopting the faith and acceptance that nature reveals to us, can we not see that a fundamental change in our reactions to everyday events would constitute a growth in consciousness?"

Furthermore, in the *The Science of Getting Rich,* Wallace Wattles states that:

"The moment you allow your mind to dwell with displeasure upon things as they are, you begin to lose ground. You fix attention upon the common, the poor, the squalid, and the mean—and your mind takes the form of these things. You will then transmit these forms or mental images to the formless. Thus, the common, the poor, the squalid, and the mean will come to you."

CHAPTER THREE
A Lesson in Soul Power

"The journey is never outward, but always and only inward toward discovery of the deeper Self."
~ *Arthur Samuel Joseph,* Vocal Power: Harnessing the Power Within

One morning, full of enthusiasm, I visited Everett Irion and told him that I had thought of a great plan to make life easier for everyone.

"You're going to love this," I told him.

His white eyebrows shot up, and his blue eyes twinkled.

I had come up with this "great" idea after only a couple of weeks of visiting him in a sunny office in the old hospital building on top of the hill at Edgar Cayce's A.R.E.

Because of the many things I'd learned from him and because my life had improved as a result of applying his suggestions, I felt encouraged to share my great revelation with him. Everett was like that. You went to see him to better understand a dream and ended up understanding life better—your life, your friend's life, even humanity's life.

On this sparkling Virginia morning, I wanted to share my idea for bettering humanity's life with the Old Elf.

No kidding, Everett looked just like an elf. He was of medium height, slender build, had white hair, white eyebrows, glistening blue eyes, a pointed chin, large ears that stuck out, and a little mouth. In addition, because he hailed from Texas, he always wore a lariat-style necktie.

When I look back on that fateful day, I cringe. It is amazing that that dear old man did not fall off his chair laughing uproariously at me and my "brilliant" idea.

But he did not. Everett was like that—safe. You knew he would only have understanding and compassion for you.

The Not-Too-Great Idea

Everett sat on his wooden high-backed chair. His eyes behind his spectacles were luminous in anticipation.

"OK," I said, "I have just discovered a wonderful way to make everyone's life better."

His eyes continued to twinkle like stars in a desert night.

"It's simple," I said. "The problem is that all of us do really stupid things that make our lives miserable. We have temper tantrums, eat too much, drink too much, say things we wish we hadn't. Some of us fantasize instead of going after life and others blame everyone for their unhappiness instead of taking the responsibility them-selves. I could go on and on. You know what I mean."

I waited to see his reaction.

He nodded.

"On top of it all," I continued, "we seem to be totally unaware of these aspects of our character that make our lives miserable."

He nodded again. His eyes looked like deep pools of azure as he waited to hear what else I had to say.

"OK," I said, "this is my great idea: The obvious solution for all our problems is to ask someone who loves us to tell us what we're doing wrong so we can change our behavior. Then we'll be happy."

Like I said earlier, the Old Elf did not even bat a white eyelash.

He smiled softly. His eyes looked quiet and kind.

"It's a great idea," he said. "But, do you think it will work?"

He waited to let his words sink in.

I knew, because he asked the question, that he did not think it would work. I felt disappointed, but I thought about it for awhile.

"I guess it won't work," I said.

I thought some more. He waited.

"After all," I continued, "even when I know my own faults, I cannot seem to stop myself from doing what I know works against me."

I thought about my years of trying to lose weight, how I often blurted out unsolicited advice, and how messy I was.

"You're right," he smiled gently.

"Why doesn't it work?" I asked. "It would be so much simpler to just look at ourselves and do what we know is the right thing. But we do not. Why? Even when I start out with the best intentions, I often end up acting in ways that are harmful to both myself and others."

"You're right," he said. "And, do you know why?"

I shook my head. "No, I haven't a clue."

"It's easy," he replied, his eyes twinkling like sunlight sparkling on a river. "You're making suggestions based on working with your conscious mind. That won't work."

"Why not?" I asked.

"It won't work," he replied, "because you are trying to make changes based on the power of your conscious mind. Your habits are under the control of your much more powerful subconscious mind."

It was then I realized that all the work I had been doing with Everett—studying my dreams, being grateful, the 40-day prayers—were all methods of working with the elusive but powerful subconscious.

The subconscious is so powerful because it contains:

- All the memories of this lifetime

- The knowledge and ability to keep your body alive with all the autonomic processes that keep your body going without your conscious control

- The psychological complexes that resulted from emotional traumas suffered during childhood

- Memories of previous lifetimes and previous existences

- A constant connection with the super-conscious or God

- That part of you that can bring about your undoing if you pretend it does not exist

- All knowledge and power because it is connected with the super-conscious or God

More Powerful than the Conscious Mind

Part of the reason the subconscious is so powerful is because it is charged with keeping the body alive. Your heartbeat, your digestion, your elimination systems, your repair systems of the body such as blood coagulation, all function entirely without your conscious control. Quite literally, your subconscious has your best interests at heart.

Another reason the subconscious is more powerful than the conscious mind is that the real you that is eternal resides there. This is the you that has reincarnated in so many different bodies and circumstances, the you that has been in a number of different life forms through the root races, the you that is really a Light Being and was originally made in the image of the Creator — pure Light and Love.

The subconscious also preserves you from emotional devastation through creating coping mechanisms. Many of these coping mechanisms were developed during your childhood to maintain your emotional survival. Some develop during your adult years when you go through emotional traumas.

Sometimes these emotional survival patterns are called psychological complexes. Sometimes they are called emotional trash or emotional baggage. Whatever you call them, the emotional survival patterns learned in childhood, or as a result of emotional trauma in adult life, often persist even when they are no longer necessary or useful. They can also work against you when your emotional survival patterns become habits that create totally inappropriate reactions in your present circumstances.

Getting to Know the Subconscious

The subconscious, by its very name ("sub" meaning "under") appears to be inaccessible, secret, and unknown to us. By the way, the word "unconscious," meaning "not conscious," is often used interchangeably with the word "subconscious" because the working of our subconscious mind seems to be not accessible, secret, and unknown to us. However, because "unconscious" can also mean that a person has lost consciousness as in being "knocked out" or "in a coma," I am using "subconscious" to mean that part of our mind that is under everyday consciousness and appears to be inaccessible to our everyday conscious mind.

Although the workings of our subconscious mind seem to be inaccessible, secret, and unknown to us, we do directly experience thoughts and images from our subconscious. It is the stuff of dreams and fantasies. We all experience them—thoughts that arise, unbidden, in our minds. Perhaps we awaken from a dream or reverie wondering, "Where did that come from?"

The answer is that it wells up from the subconscious.

That is why you do not have to go to the highest heaven or lowest hell: God or Universal Law is there with you wherever you go. You are in your soul which is connected to Universal Law. Whether you are a devoutly religious person who says that God spoke to them in prayer or meditation, or you are a just-as-devout believer in the power of nature who says that they know things through symbols, intuition, or science, the inspiration comes to you through the subconscious.

CHAPTER FOUR
The Magical 40-Day Manifestation Prayer

"Oh, Great Spirit
Whose voice I hear in the winds,
And whose breath gives life to all the world,
Hear me, I am small and weak,
I need your strength and wisdom. ..."

~Translation by Chief Yellow Lark, Lakota Sioux, 1887

The 40-Day Manifestation Prayer is my favorite prayer because it brought my husband to me. Everett Irion taught it to me.

If you have read *When We Were Gods* or *The Golden Ones*, you know that after I had the dream showing me the stranger I would marry, I saw him in real life the next day. However, I did not go running up to him saying, "Hey, guess what? You're the man of my dreams!"

On the contrary, I watched and waited and wondered, "Who could this man be that I dreamt about?"

Although I felt profoundly attracted to him, I felt afraid to approach him, fearful of rejection. I also felt sad because he did not appear to notice me at all, and I assumed that meant he would never be attracted to me.

A year went by. I forgot about the man of my dreams and went about my life.

In the meantime, I decided to try the 40-Day Manifestation Prayer Everett had taught me. I hoped it would help me find my twin soul—my other half, the soul who had been with me from the beginning of time.

You have to pray the 40-Day Manifestation Prayer consistently for 40 days. On the 39th day of praying the prayer, I walked around a corner and literally ran into the man I had dreamed about—smack, right into his chest.

After that, he noticed me. After awhile he asked me out on a date ... and eventually we married.

The concept underlying this prayer is the same as Everett's suggestion to be thankful for everything. In the case of the 40-Day Manifestation Prayer, you are not just generally thankful for whatever comes into your life. In this prayer, you specifically pray about something you really want. Similar to the "like attracts like" spiritual law of being grateful, you phrase your prayer in positive terms as if you already have whatever it is you want.

You do not say, "Take this awful thing away from me," or, "Give me this wonderful thing I want." Both of those thought patterns assume you do not have what you want. They will continue the lack in your life.

Instead, you pray with thanks as if you *already have* what you want. The 40-Day Manifestation Prayer focuses that thankfulness to bring you something you want. It also emphasizes your relationship with the Infinite by asking for what you want in the name of what you consider to be your Higher Power.

Pray in the Name of Jesus the Christ or
Your Higher Power

Since Everett derived this prayer from his understanding of Edgar Cayce's psychic readings and since Cayce was a devout Christian, it is no wonder that the prayer contains the words, "in the name of Jesus the Christ."

In over 100 readings, Cayce's spiritual source suggests that people read the promises in the 14th, 15th, 16th, and 17th chapters of the Gospel of John. In trance, after naming these Biblical chapters, Cayce would often go on to say some version of:

> "... and know that these refer to thee. In each line, in each verse, see self receiving those promises, those blessings that He has promised."

The quote is an excerpt from reading 272-8, which he gave for a 36-year-old female schoolteacher.

So, what are the promises Cayce refers to? Here they are as quoted from the *Revised Standard Version of the Bible: The New Oxford Annotated Bible with Apocrypha*:

- Jesus says in John 14:13, "Whatever you ask in my name, I will do it, that the Father may be glorified in the Son; if you ask anything in my name, I will do it."

- Then, in John 15:7 and 8, Jesus says again, "If you abide in me, and my words abide in you, ask whatever you will, and it shall be done for you. By this my Father is glorified, that you bear much fruit ..."

- Later in that Chapter, John 15:16 and 17, Jesus says, "You did not choose me, but I chose you and appointed you that you should go and bear fruit and that your fruit should abide; so that whatever you ask the Father in my name, he may give it to you."

- In John 16:23 and 24, He says yet again, "Truly, truly, I say to you, if you ask anything of the Father, he will give it to you in my name. Hitherto you have asked nothing in my name; ask, and you will receive, that your joy may be full."

- In Chapter 17 of John, Jesus assures us that he has the ability to keep His promises to those who pray in His name because He and God are one.

It can be concluded, then, that the promise is that if you ask for something in the name of Jesus the Christ, then it will be done.

Keeping that in mind, here is the 40-Day Manifestation Prayer as I learned it from Everett:

In the name of Jesus, the Christ, thank You that <u>(your</u> <u>heart's desire as if you already have it)</u>*, if it be Thy will. Amen.*

For example, I prayed:

In the name of Jesus, the Christ, thank You that I have found my twin soul, if it be Thy will. Amen.

Because I realize that many people are not comfortable with the idea of praying to Jesus, the Christ, and because I am aware that the Christ Consciousness has many names, it is acceptable to use any of the names to refer to what Christians call the Christ Consciousness.

In the following version of the prayer, I have made some suggestions for substitutions you may want to make. Basically, you are invoking the help of a Power Greater than You.

In the name of (Jesus, the Christ, the Virgin Mary, Moses, Mohammed, Buddha, My Higher Power, Krishna, Quasars and Galaxies, etc.) *thank You that* <u>(your heart's desire as if you already have it)</u>*, if it be Thy will. Amen.*

Over the years, I have also prayed it as:

Thank you, (God, G-d, the Universe, Yahweh, Mother Earth, Allah, the Creator, Vibration, Energy, Great Spirit, the Force, etc.), *in the name of* (Jesus the Christ, the Virgin Mary, Moses,

Mohammed, Buddha, My Higher Power, Krishna, Quasars and Galaxies, etc.) *that* (your heart's desire as if you already have it), *if it be Thy will. Amen.*

Make Sure the Prayer is Phrased as if You Already Have What You Want

Our subconscious mind responds so much better to the phrase, "Thank you for my twin soul," than to the phrase, "Help me, I'm so lonely," or "Don't bring another jerk into my life!"

By being negative, we court creating more loneliness or attracting another unsuitable partner.

Again, I emphasize that you make sure to phrase your heart's desire as if you already have it. If you say, for example, "I want to find my twin soul," you will be creating a constant "wanting," and will not be "finding" your twin soul, which is what you really want. Therefore, it is better to pray, "Thank you that I have found my twin soul."

In retrospect, I wish I had prayed, "that my twin soul and I live joyously in love" instead of that I had found my twin soul. Maybe we would not have had to go through so many adjustments.

End with "If It Be Thy Will"

Furthermore, you must end the prayer with the simple caveat, "if it be Thy will." You want to bring those things into your life that are in your best interest. By praying, "if it be Thy will," you leave it to a Power Greater than You to decide.

This concept is a refinement of those texts that suggest that you draw to yourself whatever you think about, visualize, and feel as if you already have what you want. With the 40-Day Manifestation Prayer you do all of that—think about, visualize, and feel as if you already have what you want—but you do one little bit more.

You ask that the Infinite or the Creative Forces add its input. Since what you want may not bring you happiness or be good for you or anybody else, this prayer leaves a place for the Universe and your Greater Self to guide you.

This can be a good thing. You may want something or someone that is not good for you. For example, that person who seems so attractive may actually be very abusive.

Or, you may not think of everything to ask. Years ago, my first husband and I wanted a better home. Unfortunately, we did not know about the 40-Day Manifestation Prayer.

Instead, we made a Vision Board of exactly the kind of home we wanted. We cut out magazine pictures and glued them together. The montage included a stream, trees, and fields because we wanted to live in the country. We were in our "back to the land" phase so we added an older home with a cold cellar for storing food as well as a wood stove for heat and a shed full of split wood. We also wanted friends and so included them in the montage.

In the end, we got everything we had wanted, which we had included in the montage. We even had a gurgling brook flowing through one part of the property. Amazingly, the property looked just like the picture we had made in our montage. We also had the most wonderful neighbors and made great friends—all characteristics we had asked for.

"So, what's the problem?" you ask.

We had not thought of all the details. Most significantly, it had not occurred to us to consider the type of landlord we would have.

What a nightmare! It turned out that our landlord, who lived only a few feet away across the road, had suffered a brain injury in an accident. He could not accept that because we paid him rent the house was ours to live in, not his. Everyday he barged into the house. Everyday he camped out in my kitchen talking to me as I made meals, cared for the children, and cleaned.

I could not get rid of him. He walked into the house without knocking. When he was not in the house, he lurked outside in the woodshed and in the barn. He talked non-stop and over and over again about the same things.

In addition, when we were away from the house, he would go into it. I knew he had been in while we were away because I could see his footsteps on the floor.

Once I contracted a virulent influenza. It was one of those viruses that give you terrible pain in your head. I had a high fever and felt afraid that my two-month-old baby might get sick as well. I feared I would lose my ability to breastfeed the baby because of the illness.

The last thing I needed was a visit from anyone, never mind a deranged old man. However, late in the evening on a cold dark winter's night, with the wind whistling and quivering against the windows of the old house, he arrived at our doorstep as I struggled with pain and fever.

My husband told the old man that he needed to go home. He was not welcome. I felt very sick and needed to be left alone. Our landlord said that he was lonely and needed to be with us. My husband insisted that the old man give us some privacy.

Although the landlord did not come into the house that night, he did not leave. In the end, because my husband would not let him into the house, the old man sat in our enclosed porch for much of the night. He was as stubborn to remove as a grape juice stain and as clingy as mold on an orange.

Because of this experience, I learned that:

- Yes, the "prayer wheel" Vision Board worked

- Yes, it got me what I wanted

- No, it did not bring me happiness because …

- No, it did not take into account those things I did not know about or think to ask for

I'm sure you can tell why I like this 40-Day Manifestation Prayer so much. It takes into account those things you do not know about or think of to ask. That is why it includes the phrase, "if it be Thy will."

I also like this 40-Day Manifestation Prayer because, with the phrase, "if it be Thy will," it invites direction from the Divine. This 40-Day Manifestation Prayer truly honors that which is greater than us.

I suspect that many people dislike the idea of, "if it be Thy will," because they do not want to lose control over their lives. They would really like to have it "My will," rather than, "Thy will."

There is also the ominous connotation of the passage in Luke 22:42 when Jesus says, "Father, if Thou art willing, remove this cup from me; nevertheless not my will, but Thine, be done," as Jesus confronts the inevitability of his crucifixion. As a result, it appears that "if it be Thy will," means that the Universe will "smite" you heartily.

Actually, "Thy will" is always for our good, even as it was for Jesus. He, by being crucified, had the opportunity to overcome death and by the manner of his death, show that he really had died. Because of this, his resurrection truly was a miracle. As painful as it was for Him, no one could say that His body had not been mortally tortured nor could they say that He hadn't really died and therefore had not really risen from the dead.

Why 40?

Everett told me that 40 was a powerful mystical number. It occurs a number of times in the Bible:

- 40 days: Jesus was seen on earth after his crucifixion.

- 40 days: Jesus spent wandering in the wilderness.

- 40 days: Jonah warned the people of Ninevah that they had 40 days to change their ways or else God would destroy their city. They repented and were spared.

- 40 days: Moses was on the mountain to talk with God and receive the Ten Commandments.

- 40 years: For Moses to find the Promised Land.

- 40 days: Goliath came before David killed him.

- 40 days and nights: God made it rain when he wanted to destroy the world and start over.

- 40 days and nights more: Noah's arc floated in the flood before he opened a window to see what the world was like.

In addition, 40 days is almost six weeks—the time many people consider it takes to create a new habit. In this case, it is a mental and spiritual habit based on the Law of Attraction.

CHAPTER FIVE
Guidelines for Using the 40-Day Manifestation Prayer

"Keep in mind that everything in this universe you can see with the naked eye and everything you cannot see, is an expression of Spirit."

~ Bob Proctor, You Were Born Rich

Remember, you have to pray this prayer for 40 days in a row. If you miss a day, you have to start all over again. For example, if you pray consecutively every day for 10 days and then miss Day 11, the next day you do *not* resume on Day 12. Instead you have to start all over again on Day One.

Feel Positive

In addition to phrasing your prayer as if you already have what you want, it is important to feel thankful, or at least positive, when you're saying this prayer. If you just say, "thank you," but feel angry or wanting, you will likely attract more that makes you feel angry or wanting. It's like the "thank you," or the appreciation, is then linked with the negative emotion you are projecting. You want the "thank you" to be linked with good feelings so that more of those good feelings will be brought into your life.

I know sometimes it can seem difficult to muster up that kind of positive feeling, especially when you think about something you really want. One trick is to think about how you will feel once you have it. That is the feeling you are after and the feeling you want to attract. Another thing you can do is to engage in something else that makes you feel really good. This other activity can give you a boost. You could make a Gratitude List, listen to uplifting music, or talk to someone who always makes you feel good (like a best friend). If there's something else that puts you in a good mood, then do that.

Believe, Be Sincere, Be Sure

Sometimes people do not get results when they undertake the 40-Day Manifestation Prayer because they do not really put their hearts into it. One woman told me that the prayer did not work for her until she really believed it. Before that, she had been saying it without sincerity. She had thought it was a silly game for her amusement rather than something real. Once she thought out the connection the words made with her subconscious, and through it to the Divine, she began to receive results.

If while you are praying you are also muttering in the back of your mind, "This will never work," then guess what? You're right. It will never work. You have just made sure of that by way of your doubting thoughts. The message you will be sending is "I really want this but it will never happen."

Instead, you need to believe, be sincere, and feel that it can happen and send the message of, "Thank you for this happening." If you can believe that what you are asking for is at least *possible*, that should be good enough.

Similarly, if you have a bunch of fears for why your request shouldn't happen or why it might be a bad idea, it can block the process of manifestation. As far as your Higher Self, God, the Universe, etc. is concerned, you clearly aren't really sure about what you want. How can the Creative Forces fulfill your request if you aren't all that sure about it yourself or even sure whether you really want it fulfilled in the first place?

It is a good idea to give your intended request careful thought. If need be, write down the things that pop into your mind for why it won't work or why it could be a bad thing. That way, you give yourself the opportunity to offer a counter viewpoint before you begin your prayer cycle. You get to list why it can work, all the good things that will come with it, and why the bad things might not happen or might actually be good things and things you can feel good about.

Be Clear, Be Specific

If you are vague about what you want, then it is very difficult to manifest what it is you're after. How can you possibly ask for what it is you want when you don't really know what it is you want? Again, it is important to give your intended prayer careful thought and be very clear about what it is you're after.

A young woman told me the amusing results of her 40-Day Manifestation Prayer. She decided to pray for her "twin flame," which is another phrase for a twin soul. She faithfully prayed the prayer for 40 consecutive days. On the 40th day, her mother presented her with two antique candlestick holders with candles in them. She had received her "twin flames."

As a result, she realized that it was not enough to merely say or write the words down. She had to also visualize her twin flame as well as *feel* as if she was already with him.

When she redid the 40-Day Manifestation Prayer, she did meet a man who was a wonderful lover, just the kind of man she wanted.

Make Your Request Reasonable

Be reasonable in your request. For example, if you expect to lose 100 pounds in six weeks, you are being unreasonable. However, you might discover a wonderful way of becoming and maintaining a slender body. During the six weeks of the 40-Day Manifestation Prayer, you might be well on your way to losing the 100 pounds, but physically it is not possible to lose that much weight in six weeks.

Likewise, you cannot expect to regrow a limb, but you might learn of a wonderful new prosthetic device that would be closer to having your own limb.

Give Your Full Attention

Although it may be tempting to try and cover as many "wishes" as possible at one time, you should really do only one prayer at a time. When you are finished with that prayer, you can move on to another prayer.

By doing only one prayer at a time, the attention from your Higher Power is focused on only that one issue. When you try to do multiple prayers simultaneously, the available energy ends up being fragmented and having less power for each issue. Often the result is that no one thing has enough attention, focus, or energy to allow manifestation to occur.

Suggestions from Everett

In addition to the recommendations already mentioned, here are some suggestions from Everett for getting the most out of your 40-Day Manifestation Prayer:

- After you pray the prayer, forget about it for that day. Allow the prayer to do its work. Enjoy yourself.

- If you are having trouble keeping your mind off the prayer, just keep saying, "Thank you, Father," or, "Thank you," to whomever or whatever represents your Higher Self.

- Do not tell anyone what your prayer is during the 40 days (or longer if you miss a day and need to start over again). You are saying the prayer. You do not want anyone else's ideas, opinions, or agendas interfering with the energy you are setting in motion.

- Do not expect any results until the 39th or 40th day. Sometimes you need to go to the 41st or 42nd day.

And remember, it must be 40 days in a row—without missing a day. As I wrote in *When We Were Gods,* when I used the 40-Day Manifestation Prayer, nothing happened until the 39th consecutive day. On that day, I literally ran into the same man I had dreamed about marrying a year earlier. I also had to do the prayer longer than just 40 days since I missed Day 22 and had to start all over.

- In an emergency, you can use 40 hours instead of 40 days.

- Keep track of the number of days (or hours). Whether you mark the days off on a calendar or you write the prayer down, you'll probably need some method to know what day you are on.

You may find, as I have, that it is easiest to write the prayer down. I like to write my 40-Day Manifestation Prayer in my dream journal. You can also keep a journal specifically for writing down the prayer. Make sure you date and number each entry in your journal. Otherwise you may skip a day and not even know it.

CHAPTER SIX

What to Expect from the 40-Day Manifestation Prayer

"For all prayer is answered. Don't tell God how to answer it."
~ Edgar Cayce Reading 4028-1

As with my experience with the 40-Day Manifestation Prayer, you may get what you prayed for … or something very close. In my case, I am not sure if my husband and I are twin souls. But according to my hypnosis sessions, we have known each other from the beginning of my time on earth. And anyway, what I really wanted was a life partner, and that is what I got.

You May Get What You *Really* Want
Instead of What You Pray For

The 40-Day Manifestation Prayer does not always produce the results you would like. It sometimes gives you something even better.

For example, I once prayed for better vision. I had meant that I did not want to wear corrective lenses anymore. As a result of that prayer, I began to see visions. But I'm still wearing glasses.

Let me give you another example out of my own life of how the 40-Day Manifestation Prayer can give you what you really want. Since I have been describing the way I met my husband, you probably expect that because my husband is "the man of my dreams" our marriage is a "marriage made in heaven." Actually, it is far from it. We have two very different personalities. Although we may have known each other from the beginning of my time on earth and have shared many lifetimes together, in this experience we have both come from very different circumstances.

When I wished for "the other half of my puzzle," I did not realize what this could mean. He truly is my opposite in life experience. Whereas I spent most of my adult life as a mother, he was always a bachelor. I had never been alone. He had always been. Although he had many girlfriends, he never lived with anyone. When I moved in with him, I brought three children, one dog, and four cats.

I naturally expected him to love that we had filled his loneliness. His life was now full of commotion, emotion, and joy. He naturally expected me to appreciate the financial security he brought me. And we both did appreciate what the other brought into the relationship.

However, neither of us realized how difficult the adjustment would be. He resented that the children and animals took so much of my time and energy away from him. I resented how much emphasis he put on his possessions. From my point of view, people and animals far outweighed a house in importance. Of course, since the house was his, he felt angry that the walls were becoming scuffed and the carpets worn. Looking at the situation with the wisdom of the years, I can see that we both needed to make a lot of adjustments and compromises.

What bothered me the most was that he seemed unwilling to work things out. I know that what bothered him the most was that, like most women, I had to talk about things too much. I think the final straw in our inability to resolve our differences centered around my need to have him tell me that he loved me.

Whenever I asked for assurance he would say, "You're wearing my ring. Isn't that enough?"

It wasn't. I needed to hear the words.

Finally, I felt so disappointed in the marriage that I prayed a 40-Day Manifestation Prayer in which I thanked God for getting me and the children our own place so I could move away from my dream man.

As the 40 days progressed, I wondered how the Universe was going to produce new living accommodations for me and the children. I was looking for housing arrangements and nothing was coming up that I could afford, or if I could afford it, it did not allow three children, a dog, and four cats.

On the 40th day John woke up in the morning and told me that he'd been having a rough time at work. He apologized for being so distant. Then he said, "I love you."

In the end, I got what I *really* wanted much more than a home of my own—a verbal affirmation of John's love for me.

Some people, instead of getting their desired results, learn something important about themselves. For example, one shy young woman prayed for a boyfriend. Within a week of starting the prayer many attractive young men entered her life. As she continued to pray, she kept waiting for them to ask her out on a date. However, by her 40th day, she realized that no matter how many gorgeous hunks the Universe brought her way, if she felt too afraid to talk with the men when they said, "Hi," there would be no relationship. She would have to learn how to reply and carry on a conversation.

Therefore, when you get to the end of your 40-Day Manifestation Prayer, should you *not* get exactly what you prayed for, please note what you *did* get.

Results Can Be Revealed in Different Ways

Not everyone receives their results or answers in the same way. Perhaps you have a dream giving you direction in your life. Someone might say something by chance that helps you to make an important decision. You could see something or hear something coincidentally that is exactly what you need to know.

One woman who organized a series of speaking engagements for me receives messages on bumper stickers or from images printed on trucks. For example, she had to make the decision whether to schedule one of my speaking tours as one large event in a single central location or a series of whistle stops at a number of smaller localities.

When she saw a cartoon image of a number of frogs (if you have read *When We Were Gods* you know why the frogs would be significant) holding hands in a row painted on the side of a delivery truck, she knew I should make a number of small puddle jumps rather than one large splash. She was right. It turned out that the smaller localities really appreciated having a speaker come to their area. In addition, the total turnout was much larger than if I had gone to only one central location.

A man I know receives his messages from television programs. When he has decisions to make he notices what turns up on the screen. He told me that all programs have a "take away" message — even sitcoms and cartoons — from the importance of friends to the need to appreciate what you already have. Whatever turns up helps him to make decisions or to support choices he's already made.

Although most results don't appear until the 39th or 49th day, sometimes people find that their lives begin to change almost as soon as they begin Day One of the prayer. This occurs most often when a person prays for a change in themselves. For example, the young lady in the earlier example who wanted a boyfriend next prayed that she would learn how to not only reply when an attractive man approached her, but also learn how to make the first move herself.

Almost as soon as she started the prayer, she began to find it so much easier to reach out to people. By the time she reached Day 40, she had overcome much of her shyness. She could see that she had the power within her to make friends. She did not have to wait for people to come up to her.

She could say, "Hi, how are you?"

And she did get asked out on a date.

You May Discover What You Need to Do

As you can see from the above example, the result of your 40-Day Manifestation Prayer may not be to receive your heart's desire on a silver platter. Instead, you may discover something you need to do to get it.

Recently I had an experience with the 40-day prayer when I did not receive what I asked for—far from it—but I did receive wonderful answers to another more pressing problem. The answer arrived in the form of things I must do. This is why I suggest that you keep an open mind to whatever may turn up.

I had been praying for an increase in my income but received good health instead ... or actually, not health delivered overnight on a platter as if I'd just touched the hem of Jesus' cloak, but health in the form of an avalanche of things to do to improve my well-being. I must admit that I had been starting to have some health issues that, if left unattended, could have led to more serious consequences. As I ended my 40-Day Manifestation Prayer, my Higher Power proclaimed that I needed to attend to health issues more than I needed to increase my income.

From my point of view, nothing much happened on the last day of my 40-Day Manifestation Prayer in which I thanked the Universe for a specific amount of income. Day 40 occurred while my husband John and I were in British Columbia, Canada, meeting with musicians who had contributed their compositions to my travel movie, *Yucatan Travel: Cancun to Chichen Itza.*

During dinner on Day 40, someone mentioned a web site that was supposed to be very helpful for planning travel in the Yucatan. I thought that maybe this was the answer to my prayers since I could possibly market *Yucatan Travel: Cancun to Chichen Itza* on that site. Nothing more happened that day that could potentially help with increasing my income.

However, on the day *after* the end of my 40-day prayer—Day 41—John and I were videotaping footage for a future movie on Atlantis. We were in Victoria, British Columbia, in Chinatown. I was using a large decorative sculpture of an earth globe to show how the earth looked during Atlantean times according to Edgar Cayce's trance source.

After filming, I rested at a coffee shop and John, ever on the prowl for a bargain, came upon an Oriental herb shop. He went in to purchase some inexpensive green tea. When he peeked at the back of the shop, he noticed a Chinese man in session with a Caucasian woman. John inquired of the shop girl if the man gave consultations on what herbs to use to improve health.

The shop girl said, "Yes."

Excited, John sought me out. He knew I had been having some symptoms that concerned me. He insisted that I needed to have a session with the man. I did.

The man suggested a number of Chinese herbs, which we took home with us. They have been very helpful.

In addition, the next day—Day 42, while flying home on the aircraft, I happened to read a magazine that described lifestyle changes based on innovative genetic testing. Furthermore, once I got home—Day 43, I came across a book I had had for years. I had not paid much attention to it. However, when I opened its pages, I found wonderful suggestions and incorporated them in my life as well.

While writing this, I remembered that the day *before* the end of my 40-day prayer for wealth—Day 39, John and I had come upon a tea shop in Richmond, British Columbia, a community south of Vancouver that is about 44 percent Chinese. Since my medical doctor in the United States had suggested I drink green tea to improve my health, John and I went into this tea shop to see what the Chinese, the originators of tea used as a beverage, had to say about green tea.

Well, were we in for a surprise! To begin, we learned that almost all "green tea" sold packaged in tea bags is no longer "green" but is old. After all, "green" means fresh. Furthermore, we learned that black tea results when green tea leaves are fermented.

Next, we learned that the benefits in green tea are actually destroyed if you make green tea using boiling water. That also makes sense since both vitamin C and the B vitamins are destroyed by high heat. Brewing with boiling water also makes green tea taste bitter. The proprietor of the shop taught us the correct temperature with which to brew green tea. Of course, we bought a canister of genuine green tea which has a delightful earthy fragrance that I love.

We also had the wonderful opportunity to experience the Chinese tea ceremony which uses a tiny unglazed clay teapot to brew the leaves, a "mixer" teapot, "sniffer" cups with which to enjoy the aroma, and lovely little ceramic teacups.

Not surprisingly, we also bought a number of little tea sets. I have been drinking the delightful aromatic beverage since returning home. It is so much fun to conduct the tea ceremony everyday knowing I am preparing green tea in the proper manner.

By implementing the flood of suggestions that "turned up" the days before and after I ended my 40-day prayer, my health has steadily improved.

Who would have thought that a prayer for wealth would have cured symptoms and brought vitality and well-being ... unless to have greater wealth, a person needs more vitality to pursue a greater income!

Or, could it be that health is the greatest wealth? As Lao Tzu, who is considered the founder of the Taoist religion, says, "Health is the greatest possession."

I don't know. I do know that the initial disappointment I felt over not getting what I asked for has given way to a profound gratitude for that Power, Greater than Myself, that had my best interests at heart and knew, better than I did, what was best for me.

Therefore, at the end of your 40-Day Manifestation Prayer, notice the things that come your way. Do not assume that just because you receive something that is *not* what you asked for that your 40-day prayer did not work. It could be that what you *did* receive is actually a gift from the Universe of what you *really* need. In addition, you may not immediately understand how it is that what you did receive was an answer to your prayers. The understanding may follow after you implement the suggestions that came your way.

In addition, notice not only what comes to you on a silver platter but also the suggestions of activities or lifestyle changes you can do that may bring improvement into your life. After all, once you have spent 40 consecutive days asking for the Universe's help, it is important that if you receive an opportunity to put something into action, you do your part and do whatever needs to be done.

Other Results from the 40-Day Manifestation Prayer

Obviously, if you do not finish 40 consecutive days, do not expect the same results as you would get if you do finish the prayer. Remember, if you miss a day and do not start from the beginning, thinking that it won't matter, it will. That's the whole purpose of the 40-day prayer—that you maintain the same belief for that magical Biblical number of 40 days, one after another without a break, like a long, strong chain. You know that a chain will not work if a link is missing. It is the same with the 40-day prayer. All the days must be linked to one another.

In addition, for some people the phrase, "if it be Thy will," keeps them from either saying the prayer or believing in it. They, perhaps, have grown up with an especially repressive religious experience and fear that fire and brimstone may be God's will for them. They feel afraid of putting themselves in the hands of a repressive God. They need to see that the repression came from the religious organization they grew up with, not from the Creator, maker of the heavens and the cosmos.

There are also people who balk at "if it be Thy will," because they do not believe in a personal God. They can understand the power of nature and the intricate inter-relationships of science, but they perceive "believers" as misguided individuals who live in a fantasy world believing that a grandfatherly old man with a beard looks after them. Sometimes nothing can open their minds until they have a personal experience of the Divine in their lives. However, some people in this group are so strong in their belief that nothing exists but the physical that even if an angel appeared to them they would explain it away as a hallucination.

If this is how you feel, you have my empathy because I have been struggling with my own disbelief of the things that have appeared to me. It is very normal to fight against anything new. You feel as if, should you accept what you experienced, your whole life is going to change.

And, as a dear family friend used to say, "Change is deadly."

How do I handle my own disbelief? I do research. That means talking to people who have had similar experiences, reading books, and attending seminars. In addition, I travel to find confirmation of some of the concepts that have come to me. It took me years to feel comfortable with "Thy will" instead of my will.

CHAPTER SEVEN
Powerful Prayers

For myself, I am an optimist — it does not seem to be much use being anything else.

~ *Winston Churchill*

For most people prayers are spoken in places of worship and at bedtime. However, these prayers may be what Mark Twain's Recording Angel calls "Public Prayers" or "Sunday School Prayers of Professional Christians." In Twain's short story, "Letter to the Earth," the Recording Angel credits these prayers as "words ... according to number uttered within certain limits of time" most of which account for "wind." In the story, it is only the "Secret Supplications of the Heart" that count as true prayer.

Twain is making the point that no matter what type of prayers we may make — whether the centering affirmation of meditation, the sincere supplication for help on our knees, or the genuine request of the 40-Day Manifestation Prayer — the only ones that really matter are the prayers that come from the heart.

Positive Prayers

It is also important that your prayers be phrased as positively as possible because the subconscious works the best with the positive. In addition, both adults and children respond best to positively phrased suggestions. However, children, who have not yet fully emerged out of their subconscious to form their own conscious minds, are especially responsive to positive requests rather than negative commands, even in their waking life.

Here is a lovely true story that illustrates how well positive suggestions work. This story demonstrates beautifully the power of positive, rather than negative, ways of phrasing requests. Even though it is a story about children, because children, unlike adults, are still deeply connected to their subconscious minds, it is a story showing how the subconscious mind responds to suggestions. It also demonstrates how positive ideas are more likely to create what you want.

Many years ago, I used to meet with a girlfriend and her two children once a week for breakfast at a local motel restaurant. We knew that the children would be finished with their breakfasts in a flash and would want to play. However, we would want to eat in a leisurely manner and talk.

Unfortunately, the motel grounds included an in-ground pool that did not have a fence around it. All of the children were excellent swimmers, but we didn't want them going swimming on this trip. We could see the pool from our booth in the restaurant and could run out and help anyone who might fall either into the pool or on the cement. We could also run and discipline anyone that may decide to go in the water even though they weren't given permission to do so. Even so, we preferred that they stay away from the water while they played.

At the time, I had been experimenting with positive instructions and knew that if I told the children that they were *not* to go near the pool, paradoxically, their interest would be piqued, and they'd want to explore the pool more than if I had not mentioned the pool at all. It would be as if their subconscious only heard, "Go near the pool," totally discounting the "not." Similarly, if I said, "Go ahead and play but don't get into trouble," they would have no other direction than the word, "trouble" and, therefore, could easily find it.

As a result, I took the five children on a tour of the area. They ranged in age from about five to ten years old. I said nothing about the pool. Instead, I showed them how they could play on the lawn chairs and use the tables around the pool to play. There were stairs leading around a patio surrounded with flowering plants. I took them up the stairs and all around the patio telling them this was a wonderful area for running and playing.

I still said nothing about the pool. I did not look at it nor did I mention it. Neither did I say anything about keeping away from the pool nor that I would be angry if they disobeyed me nor that I would withhold a promised treat if they went near the pool nor that they could drown if they fell in. I only told them where they could play and how wonderful these play areas were.

My suggestions complete, I wished all the children a happy play time and went back into the restaurant to sit down and talk with my girlfriend. We watched the children through the window. They never even came close to the pool. We had no fear of them stooping to put a finger in the water. They only played on the lawn chairs, the patio, and the grass. Through the window, we could hear their squeals of delight and laughter as they played. They had a marvelous time and the both of us mothers felt warm and loving toward them because they were so happy frolicking with their friends.

Recently my grown daughters and I were reminiscing about their childhood and this incident came up in the discussion. Evidently, the younger had asked her older sister, "Can we put our fingers in the water?"

They had both thought for a minute and then remembered, "No, Mommy didn't say we could play in the pool." Their young minds, much more attune with their subconscious, responded perfectly to the positive suggestions.

However, it is important to keep in mind that phrasing prayers, instructions, and requests in a positive manner applies to more than just children. I have seen phrasing our words in a positive manner work for all ages of people.

For example, you've probably experienced yourself that when you see a sign that says, "Wet Paint. Do Not Touch," most people really want to touch the paint. It is as if our subconscious mind does not see the, "Not" and instead sees a command, "Wet Paint. Do Touch." Maybe a better sign would be "Wet Paint. It will be dry when the sign is gone," or, for a chair, the sign could read, "Wet Paint, Sit Elsewhere." In both of the latter signs, there is only a bland statement with no mention of touching. A sign like the latter one will likely dissuade more people from getting paint on themselves.

Here's another one. Instead of saying, "Don't forget," wouldn't it be better to say, "Remember?" Or think of the negative connotations in the word "deadline." A friend of mine has taken "deadline" out of her vocabulary and instead uses "due date."

All these examples illustrate the power of our subconscious in our lives and how to work with it in a more effective manner by phrasing statements in a positive manner—whether you are doing a 40-day prayer or communicating in everyday usage.

Although adults and children alike benefit from positive suggestions, as mentioned previously, children are especially vulnerable to the effects of negative communications since they still operate largely out of their subconscious mind and have not yet developed a strong conscious mind.

I see it so pervasively in our culture when parents and people caring for children instruct children to, "Don't do that." What else does the child know to do but just what they have been told not to do? Wouldn't a better command be, "Please do this."

A girlfriend of mine recently reminded me of a story about her daughter, whom I used to care for during the time I homeschooled my children. It had just rained and naturally all the children were fascinated with the puddles. However, I needed them to keep dry. My friend had been saying to her daughter, "Don't step in the puddles." This was obviously not working. Instead, I said to her daughter, "It's OK if you walk around the puddles." And then, the girl made a game of walking around all the puddles. It worked!

Like this young girl, our subconscious appears to be open to suggestion. Therefore, it would be more effective to make suggestions to the subconscious in a positive manner rather than in a negative manner.

As a result, when you choose or create your prayers, be sure that they are constructed positively and are in some way open to the wisdom of God, Universal Law, or the super-conscious.

As has been mentioned earlier, the 40-Day Manifestation Prayer is a good example of a positive prayer:

> *In the name of Jesus, the Christ, thank You that (your*
> *heart's desire as if you already have it), if it be Thy*
> *will. Amen.*

CHAPTER EIGHT
Making Wise Choices

"For, know that each soul constantly meets its own self. No problem may be run away from. Meet it now!"

~ Edgar Cayce Reading 1204-3

Everett also taught me how to make choices based on soul direction. At the time, I had to choose between one of two jobs that had been offered to me. In both cases, they were opportunities that I really wanted. I came to Everett for help in choosing which of these dream jobs I should take.

In one case, the head of the A.R.E.'s Study Group Department had asked me to work for her. I had not even applied for the job. Instead, she had telephoned me, met with me, and had taken me out for lunch. I had never before been wooed like this for a job.

Furthermore, I loved participating in Cayce's Search for God study groups. It was a dream job for me. My life had improved so much from my association with like-minded people and from applying the concepts in the Cayce readings. I had attended study groups in different parts of the country and Canada for many years. I had also started a couple of study groups. This job would have been a natural for me.

The other job opportunity was in a completely different sphere of life. You could say that I am a National Air and Space Association (N.A.S.A.) groupie. I have great respect for America's space program and N.A.S.A.

Therefore, when I saw that N.A.S.A. Langley Research Center in Hampton, Virginia, was within driving distance of my new home in Virginia Beach, I wanted to visit the facility. At the time, I belonged to National Presswomen so I called up a member of that organization who worked at N.A.S.A. Langley's Office of Public Affairs.

As a way of getting to know her, I brought examples of some of my work, which included published articles and photography. In one of those amazing coincidences, it turned out that she was the N.A.S.A. representative for a contractor who was looking for a photojournalist that would work with Langley's Office of Public Affairs. She recommended me for the job. I had to compete with many people for it, but, in the end, I was the one offered the position.

I could hardly believe my good fortune—two magnificent opportunities.

"Which one should I choose?" I asked Everett.

"Which one has the most energy?" he asked me.

"What do you mean?" I asked him.

"Well, how do you feel about A.R.E.?"

"I love it."

"Any problems?"

"Well, my first husband worked at A.R.E., so I know it is not perfect."

"What about N.A.S.A.?"

"Oh, Everett," I replied. "I'm terrified to work at N.A.S.A. It's Atlantis all over again!"

Even before I went for the hypnotherapy sessions that brought me face-to-face with my memories of Atlantis, I had begun to have disturbing dreams of my experiences during that powerful, technologically-advanced time.

"Well, my dear," said Everett smiling at me with kind eyes, "I guess you'd best go face it then."

And that's how I ended up at N.A.S.A.

Therefore, when you have a difficult decision to make, one factor to consider among the many other factors could be the amount of emotional and soul energy each of the choices presents for you. The better choice may not be the one that is the easiest or most pleasant, but the one that holds the most energy for you.

CHAPTER NINE
The Profound 40-Day Forgiveness Prayer

"It is by forgiving that one is forgiven."

~ *Mother Teresa*

The 40-Day Forgiveness Prayer is another gem Everett taught me. It uses the concept that our thoughts become messages that go out to the Universe. This prayer can help to free you from guilt, fear, and resentment of someone who has hurt you or someone you have hurt.

Because your issues are with the person and not with God, you pray to the person, not to God. You also pray to yourself.

Everett's 40-Day Forgiveness Prayer was published in his column in the September/October 1985 issue of *Venture Inward*, the A.R.E.'s membership magazine. In his column, Everett described how and why he created this prayer.

He said that a man who had a terminal illness came to see him. The man had only six months to live. The man said that he believed that when he died, he would go to hell, because he had hurt his wife so much by his actions that led to their divorce.

The man also brought Everett a dream to discuss. When Everett and the man interpreted the dream, it seemed that the dream was about the man's unresolved feelings of guilt toward his ex-wife and his divorce.

As a solution to the man's quandary, Everett suggested that the man go to his ex-wife, ask for her forgiveness, and thank her for all she had done for him. However, the man explained that his ex-wife was dead so he could not do that.

Everett asked the man if he believed in an afterlife and reincarnation. The man said, "Yes," and that he believed his wife still existed even though her body had died.

Everett then requested that the man come back the next day. That night, Everett asked his subconscious to come up with a solution that would help this man with his problem. Everett had a dream that resulted in the 40-Day Forgiveness Prayer.

The next morning, Everett told the man how to pray this prayer. Neither Everett nor the man knew what to expect from using it.

However, a year later, Everett heard from the man. Remember, the man had a fatal disease and had been given only six months to live. He was still alive a year later and doing well.

The man said that Everett had healed him. Everett countered that the prayer had healed him. By using the prayer, the man had healed the unresolved conflict within him that had led to his illness.

How to Use the 40-Day Forgiveness Prayer

Like the 40-Day Manifestation Prayer, you must pray this prayer everyday for 40 days in a row. If you miss a day, you have to start over again.

In addition, because this prayer works between your subconscious and the person's subconscious, Everett suggests that you use both of your middle names. The middle name is a person's hidden or subconscious name. Of course, if you or the person do not use your first names, as in J. Everett Irion, then use the person's first name if you know it. It is preferable to use the hidden name because it more easily resonates with the hidden or subconscious mind.

If you do not know the person's middle name—or even their first name—use whatever name you know them by even if it is "the person who stole my flower vase" or "the person who shoved me on the escalator."

The prayer is:

(Name of the person you want to forgive or be forgiven by), *I am praying to you.*

Thank you, (name of the person you want to forgive or be forgiven by), *for doing to me all that you have done.*

Forgive me, (name of the person you want to forgive or be forgiven by), *for all that I have done to you.*

(Your own name), *I am praying to you.*

Thank you, (your own name), for doing to me all that you have done.

Forgive me, (your own name), for all that I have done to you.

Experiences with the 40-Day
Forgiveness Prayer

A young woman told me about her experience with the 40-Day Forgiveness Prayer. Her story illustrates the amazing power of this prayer and also the unpredictability of the subconscious.

She wanted to forgive her grandmother. The girl had been conceived out-of-wedlock while her parents were still in high school. Even though it was not the girl's fault, her grandmother blamed her and treated her coldly and critically her whole life. The grandmother's treatment of the girl wounded the young woman's heart.

Over and over again the young woman had tried to forgive her grandmother. She tried to understand the situation from the grandmother's point of view — the shame the grandmother must have felt at her daughter's unexpected pregnancy.

The young woman tried to feel better about herself by researching the many successful and important people throughout history who had been conceived out-of-wedlock. But no matter what she did, the young woman still felt hurt. She also deeply resented her grandmother's continuing cold and unfair treatment of her.

When the young woman began the 40-Day Forgiveness Prayer, she did so with the sole purpose of freeing herself of the resentment she felt for her grandmother's unfair treatment of her. By chance, on the 40th day, her grandmother came to visit. Entirely out of character, the old woman proclaimed her love for the girl and asked the girl to forgive her for the bad treatment the grandmother had inflicted upon the girl throughout all those years of her young life.

The young woman only expected to be able to forgive her grandmother. It was such a wonderful gift that her grandmother declared her love for the girl and asked for the *girl's* forgiveness.

Another woman told me about her experience with the 40-Day Forgiveness Prayer. She had approached me at the end of one of my day-long seminars. She began to tell me about this terrible situation she found herself in. It had to do with abuse and her betrayal by a family member. I am no psychologist. Therefore, I do not counsel people when they come to me with difficult relationship problems. However, I do know the 40-Day Forgiveness Prayer.

Before she could begin to describe the details of her situation, I gently interrupted her to tell her that the best suggestion I could make was that she try the 40-Day Forgiveness Prayer.

You can imagine my surprise when, eight months later, she turned up at another one of my seminars in a town which was a three-hour drive away from the town where I had originally met her.

She told me that she had to attend another one of my seminars even if it meant driving three hours to an unfamiliar city. She had been so happy with the outcome of her first one.

She also wanted to tell me about the wonderful results of her 40-Day Forgiveness Prayer. She had resolved her difficulties with her relative.

However, she said that it had not been easy. During the 40 long days of the prayer, she had had to confront her own mistakes in the relationship, including that she had allowed the abusive situation to develop between her and her relative. Nonetheless, in her opinion, the prayer had worked better than therapy. She also told me that she had used the 40-Day Forgiveness Prayer for a number of people in her life because she found it to be so effective.

CHAPTER TEN
Free Yourself of Resentment

"Man's enemies are not demons, but human beings like himself."

~ Lao Tzu

Not surprisingly, since Everett believed we would benefit from being thankful for even the difficult things in our lives, he had a prayer to pray for those people we hate and who have despicably used us.

Everett showed me an article about a man who had been detained in one of Hitler's concentration camps. It was called, "Overcoming Hatred with Love."

Should you want to read the original article in its entirety, I have since found it on the internet. It's a wonderful story: www.peacepilgrim.com/FoPP/newsletter/nl01.htm# OVERCOMING

If you know the story about the concentration camps during World War II, you know that during the war many people in the Allied countries of the United Kingdom, the United States, Canada, France, and the Scandinavian countries were unaware of the extent of the genocide perpetrated on millions of innocent people by Hitler's

Secret Service. Many German people also did not know that Hitler's military organization systematically murdered millions of Jews, gypsies, and ordinary German people who disagreed with Hitler.

However, when the Allied Powers liberated the concentration camps, they learned of the horrors that had been carried out there. They found many severely emaciated people who had barely managed to survive. They learned of the "ovens" that had murdered millions of people. They heard stories of families torn apart, women used in sexual experiments, and children destroyed. Six million Jews, among them 1,500,000 children, lost their lives in the concentration camps.

Everett told me of one man the Allies discovered. They assumed he had to be a new inmate in the concentration camp because he looked so healthy and hearty in comparison to so many of his fellow prisoners who had sunken dismal-looking faces full of despair. However, the Allies discovered that this man had actually been captured and imprisoned close to the beginning of the war. He had been in a concentration camp for almost six years. He should have been dead.

They wondered why he looked so good and assumed that he must have had a relatively easy experience. Probably he had not been separated from his loved ones and so did not crumble from rage or despair.

Soon they learned his story. It turned out that the man had every reason to hate those who had incarcerated him. He had lost every single member of his family. In fact, they had been executed before his very own eyes.

The man had been a lawyer. He said that he had seen what hate could do to people's minds and bodies. Therefore, he decided that if he hated his captors he would be no better than those who killed his loved ones. And so he decided that he would love every person he encountered for the rest of his life.

The liberating army learned that people in the camp felt drawn to the prisoner who had lost so much but who refused to ruin his life with resentment. Both prisoners and guards turned to him. Because of the man's outlook, the guards gave him responsibilities with the other prisoners. The love that shone through this man saved not only his life but also his health. It also gave him joy.

This man's story is a lesson and an example to all of us. His ability to choose love over hate shows us the importance of dropping resentment and living in love. Unfortunately, for most of us, this is not an easy thing to do.

I do not know if I could be as valiant as this man was. For the most part, I have trouble rising above petty grievances in daily interactions with family, friends, and neighbors.

However, this man, a silent and unknown hero, is certainly a model for all of us to strive toward—for our own sake. He learned to love—no, he *decided* to love—even those who had despicably used and abused him.

"What?" you say. "But, I can't pray for those who despicably use me. I hate them for what they've done or are doing to me."

This is not to say that you should allow people to misuse you or that you should not feel angry when you are wronged. Anger is a natural human emotion that helps you to protect yourself. It also helps you to know what you like and do not like and motivates you to action.

By hate, Everett meant that long-standing resentment that ruins your every waking hour. This is the hate that will destroy *you*. Everett suggested using the following prayer to free yourself:

> *Beloved Savior,* (name of person you hate) *is Thine as I am Thine. Make it right between us. Amen.*

What to Expect from the
Prayer to Free You of Resentment

I do not know if you need to pray this prayer for 40 days like Everett's other prayers. He did not mention it in terms of a 40-day prayer. It would probably help because a long, deep-seated resentment will likely need a consistent and contracted new mental habit to change it. You might also want to use the 40-Day Forgiveness Prayer to help you with a long-standing resentment that's hurting your health and happiness.

By the way, do not assume that the result of this prayer should be that you will suddenly feel a loving warmth for someone who has deeply hurt you. It might be that you will finally be able to stop that squirrel cage, that goes around and around in your mind, of recycling recriminations against the person. Or you may finally be able to understand the person's actions based upon their devastating childhood.

It doesn't necessarily mean you'll suddenly be hugging and kissing them. This person may be dangerous, deranged, psychotic, or a sociopath. Or like Miss Marple in one of Agatha Christie's murder mystery novels, you may recognize evil in the person's actions. On the other hand, they may be a well-meaning person who, because of the pressures of their life, made a mistake out of frustration.

Nonetheless, it does not matter why they did what they did to you. Your goal is to free *yourself* of the resentment you feel against someone who has hurt you or despicably used you.

This is not about the person who hurt you. It is about *you.*

As I wrote in *When We Were Gods,* when the hypno-therapist asked me while I was deeply hypnotized how we should prepare for earth upheavals, I responded, "There's no better preparation than to love. Love those who despicably use you. Pray to the angels, or your Guides, or Christ—whoever you believe in—to help you to love, for your own sake." Then I repeated more quietly and with depth, "For your own sake.'"

At the time I wrote the above words, I did not really understand why loving those who despicably used you could be good "for your own sake" as preparation for earth upheavals. As far as I was concerned, the best way to prepare for earth changes was to "store food, have a non-electric water source, and live in safety lands."

For years I kept a large organic garden, raised chickens, and kept a pantry full of canned foods I had processed with the harvest out of my garden. I don't anymore. The gardening, animal husbandry, and food processing took a long time and kept me from my purpose.

In *When We Were Gods*, I had felt threatened by the unusual information that had come through me while hypnotized. I felt panicked when I had been told by the Christ Consciousness that my purpose was to share the information that had come through me—information I could hardly understand myself—never mind share it with anyone else.

While hypnotized, I then consoled myself by saying that I could accept the information in the subconscious mind but that consciously it would take awhile.

It has been awhile. Perhaps, I am finally able to begin to understand why we should love those that despicably used us "for our own sake." It is because the bitterness and the resentment hurts us more than it hurts them. If we do not release the resentment, we are victimized twice—once by our aggressors and once again by ourselves.

I love the following quote by Thich Nhat Hanh, a Vietnamese Zen Buddhist monk now exiled in France. It helps me to see how to love those who have despicably used us:

> "When we come into contact with the other person, our thoughts and actions should express our mind of compassion, even if that person says and does things that are not easy to accept. We practice in this way until we see clearly that our love is not contingent upon the other person being lovable."

CHAPTER ELEVEN
The Paradox of the Subconscious

"They say that God is everywhere, and yet we always think of Him as somewhat of a recluse."

~Emily Dickinson

The most important thing to know in working with the subconscious is what I call the Paradox of the Subconscious. Unlike the step-by-step world of the physical, you cannot *make* things happen with the subconscious. You cannot get in your car and get what you want from your subconscious. You cannot go to a store and buy what you want. You cannot put so many ingredients together, like in a recipe, and produce what you want.

There is always an element of paradox. What does paradox mean? A computer thesaurus search comes up with "inconsistency, absurdity, irony, contradiction, impossibility and illogicality." An online search produces a definition from Princeton University, "A statement that contradicts itself." Webster's dictionary defines paradox as, "A statement which seems to oppose common sense or contradicts itself, but is perhaps true."

For me, paradox means that instead of trying harder, you let go: Let go and let God. Let go and let your Higher Self take over. Instead of fighting to become stronger, you turn the other cheek, because restraint requires an even greater strength than brute force. Instead of going out and getting it, you stay home — the story of going all around the world looking for a treasure and finding it in your own backyard.

When working with the subconscious, things do not proceed in a straight line. You do not necessarily go from here to there. You may diligently pray and meditate every day, but the result may only be sleep. Instead of experiencing joy from accomplishment, joy may come from suffering — the suffering of releasing past sorrows. Instead of curing overweight, you may connect with memories of the fabulous world of Atlantis, a topic you have found phenomenally fascinating.

Therefore, although you may do all these exercises or other techniques and disciplines, the outcome is unpredictable. It is because the exercises are done consciously while the results come from the subconscious. As a result, the end product may not be what you consciously set out to find or accomplish. However, the outcomes will be exactly what your eternal Light Self wants for you, and the outcomes will likely bring you greater joy, knowledge, or peace than you would have known to seek.

The Paradoxical Nature of the Subconscious

Although, in the conscious mind, which primarily deals with the physical, the way you undertake something is to pursue it step-by-step as you would with a recipe, with the subconscious mind, sometimes the way you get ahead is by going backward.

For example, who has not had the experience of wanting something very much, say, an intimate relationship, but the more you want it, the more it seems to elude you. Haven't you heard people say that they finally gave up and decided to concentrate on their careers, and that's just when the man or woman of their dreams turned up?

What about the many people who desire a child but fail over and over again in their attempts to conceive? Then they give up, adopt a child, and soon afterward they become pregnant.

That is what it is like with the subconscious. There is something paradoxical about how the subconscious operates. This is the reason it is so difficult to work with matters relating to the subconscious. We are taught step-by-step methods for assimilating information, training the body, and acquiring skills. We are taught that to get ahead, we need to follow a certain method and that if we do, we will get predictable results.

However, with the subconscious, results may come from unexpected places and in unexpected ways. A good example of the paradoxical nature of the subconscious is Grace.

CHAPTER TWELEVE
Grace

"There has been and is ever the promise to every soul that He, thy Father, thy God, will meet thee in thy holy temple."

~ *Edgar Cayce Reading 877-2*

With Grace, you do nothing. Grace comes to you. It is like an awakening. For example, you wake up one day and you love someone who has hurt you. You may have spent years in therapy or years searching, but no matter how hard you tried, you were never able to fully free yourself from the fear and hate you carried around with you because of what this person had done to you. And then, one day, you wake up and find out you no longer hate or fear the person. You are free. You do not know why or how, but at last, the person who hurt you or disappointed you is just another human being. That is Grace.

A good example of Grace is the story in the chapter on the 40-Day Forgiveness Prayer. The young woman prayed to be able to forgive her grandmother. Not only did the young woman receive the ability to forgive her grand-mother for her harsh treatment, but the girl also received the extra, unexpected gift of the grandmother's proclamation of love and the grandmother's request for forgiveness. That is Grace. You get something you really want, but often you were not asking for it nor did you even know to ask for it.

Conversely, you may have been doing all kinds of things ahead of time—praying, meditating, working with dreams, attending seminars, talking about the situation with friends, trying to work things out with the person, going into therapy, moving away from the problem, filling your life with a positive knowingness—to try and resolve the problem. However, nothing you were doing seemed to work. Then one day, Grace happens, and the long-standing problem is no more. It has resolved itself. You are free.

Grace and the Subconscious

Grace is the answer to the question I brought to Everett. If you remember, I thought I could bring myself happiness by making myself change. I was trying to change by using my conscious mind. However, Everett showed me that the subconscious is much more powerful and that complexes formed during childhood, or karmic patterns from past lives, are often more powerful than all the best conscious intentions in the world.

Everett showed me that Grace occurs when the subconscious steps in to change you, change the situation, give you what you want, and make your life better.

Grace is the physical manifestation of the subconscious in all its power. You are forgiven. You are healed. You love.

When the Universe gives its answers to your request, that is Grace. Grace is when God responds. It may not be exactly what you asked for or what you expected, but it is what the Universe, your subconscious, knows is what you really want. When you have consistently and persistently maintained positive thoughts and feelings that your request will be fulfilled, Grace is the gift you receive when your request is answered in the way that your subconscious knows is best. Grace is as much a law of the Universe as the Law of Attraction.

Grace and Bliss

The reason Grace is especially responsive when you are filled with joy and happiness is because the soul is, in its essence, bliss. Therefore, when you "go with your bliss," you more closely align with the spiritual.

As I wrote in *When We Were Gods* and *Arrival of the Gods in Egypt*, my memories of the vibrational state was sheer and utter bliss. The vibrational state was a time in my soul's far distant past when I was a pure Light Being and had not yet become trapped in the physical.

For Spirit, every encounter is filled with appreciation and joy. There is no knowledge of good and evil. It is all One—many different experiences but all of them wonderful.

When Grace operates in your life, the most powerful part of your subconscious, the super-conscious, which is connected with the Creator and Universal Law, manifests in the physical. Grace transforms the hurts, misconceptions, and negative patterns of this life and past lives, so your life is healed.

Grace and the Paradoxical Nature
of the Subconscious

Grace is the ultimate paradox of the subconscious. You cannot make it happen. In fact, having to *have* something can actually push it away. It would be the same as exercising a broken leg to make it heal. Exercise will only make it worse.

Patience is an important attribute of Grace. And, although to most of us the word patience means that something will take a long time, it also means that we cannot cause it to happen.

It is the same thing as waiting for a fracture to heal. We do not make it happen. It happens to us. We can set the bones, but we have to trust in the natural healing inherent in our bodies to produce the result. Many religions call this ability to wait "faith."

Getting Ready for Grace

So, how does one let go of the need to be well, happy, or loved when it hurts so much to do without? One way it sometimes comes about is to do all one can do—to do everything one knows to do, to cry, to pray, to stomp, to scream, to beg, to dream, to bargain, to follow your bliss, to allow humility to clean us, etc. Because only by doing everything we know how to do will we get to the place where we finally say, "I cannot do any more."

And then ... you let go.

Although I previously discussed using positive wording accompanied with blissful feelings in our prayers, let me contradict myself and say that sometimes it is necessary to get to rock bottom. Sometimes getting to rock bottom is what it takes to accept the reality of a situation. These are the times when you pray while on your knees, crying, curled up in a ball on the floor.

Or as Abraham Lincoln once said, "I have been driven many times to my knees by the overwhelming conviction that I had nowhere else to go."

This is when you are at your end, when you have tried all you know, when there is truly no place else to go. You sob for help, you feel all the hurt of your present circumstances ... you finally give up trying. These are the prayers that finally lead to your letting go.

There are some situations that require that type of letting go before you can allow the Universe to step in and help you. For example, in the movie and book *The Secret*, the author Rhonda Byrne did not receive the Wallace Wattle book that helped her so much until she had hit rock bottom. Her father had died, her relationships were in turmoil, and her financial advisers were telling her she was about to lose her business. She had hit bottom.

Possibly one advantage of hitting bottom is that it makes us open to ideas, suggestions, and synchronicities that come our way. A synchronicity is a concept first described by the Swiss psychologist Carl Gustav Jung to explain two events that are not causally related, but they come together in a meaningful way.

Perhaps, if Byrne had not been in such a difficult situation, she may not have taken the time to open the book, *The Science of Getting Rich* by Wallace D. Wattles, that her daughter gave her. Or, she may have only briefly scanned through it instead of studying it carefully and applying the wisdom within its pages as she did.

I'm sure you can think of the many opportunities and words of wisdom from helpful people that you have let pass without assimilating them into your life because you simply were not yet ready.

In my situation, I likely would not have been willing to approach the stranger I had dreamt would become my husband if I had not been through such a challenging first marriage and a heart-wrenching divorce. I know I would have never gone to a hypnotherapist—which led to my memories of Atlantis—if I had not had the hormonal imbalance.

On the other hand, Grace can seem to come from nowhere, with no real previous conscious attempts to fix an issue. One day, it just happens. Resentment, fear, hurt, hatred, etc. is gone. You don't know where it went or how it happened, it just did.

Grace Can Be Instantaneous

Here's a lovely example of Grace. At one time, our family had an outbreak of warts. Some of us successfully used over-the-counter wart removal remedies. For others, it was the baking soda/castor oil preparation suggested in the Cayce readings that worked. One of the children's warts disappeared over a period of a week after our doctor paid him a penny for each of his warts. One of the adults cut out the warts with a knife. Each of us experienced our healing in our own way.

But one little girl could not get rid of her warts no matter what she did. And, I was especially concerned because she had some on her face, including one on her lip and another on her eyelid. The doctor was able to cut the small long wart off her eyelid. All the rest of the warts stubbornly remained, and every few days another would appear.

One night we had a little talk as she fell asleep. We had been praying that God would help us to find a way to remove the warts from her. However, this night I discovered that, because of that prayer, she thought God had given her the warts.

"Oh no," I told her, "it is *your* body that is making the warts. *Your* skin cells are making the warts, not God."

So that night her prayer changed. Instead she said, "Please God, I made these warts. I don't know why or how, but I did it to myself. I have tried everything I know to make them go away, and they won't. Please help me. Thank you for healing me."

As she fell asleep, I hoped that we would soon find something that would work for her. I hoped that her prayer would direct us to some kind of lotion, treatment, healer, or regimen that would help her body to change the cells that had become warts back to normal tissue.

The next morning when she awoke, the wart on her lip was gone. The rest disappeared within a few days.

That's Grace!

Best Wishes on Your Spiritual Journey

I hope that the suggestions within these pages will be of help to you. I encourage you to try various activities that appeal to you. In the appendix I have listed the 40-Day Manifestation Prayer, the 40-Day Forgiveness Prayer, and the Prayer to Free You of Resentment.

May God bless and keep you.

Appendix

Following, please find the 40-Day Manifestation Prayer, the 40-Day Forgiveness Prayer, and the Prayer to Free You of Resentment. I suggest you do only one prayer at a time. Let the energy work simply and directly.

The 40-Day Manifestation Prayer

In the name of   (Jesus, the Christ, the Virgin Mary, Moses, Mohammed, Buddha, Krishna, Quasars and Galaxies, My Higher Power, etc.)

thank you that I have   (your heart's desire as if you already have it)

if it be Thy will. Amen.

Over the years, I have also phrased the
40-Day Manifestation Prayer as follows:

Thank you,   (God, G-d, the Universe, Yahweh, Mother Earth, Allah, the Creator, Vibration, Energy, Great Spirit, the Force, etc.)

in the name of   (Jesus, the Christ, the Virgin Mary, Moses, Mohammed, Buddha, Krishna, Quasars and Galaxies, My Higher Power, etc.)

that   (your heart's desire as if you already have it.)

if it be Thy will. Amen.

The 40-Day Forgiveness Prayer

_____ (Name of person you want to forgive or be forgiven by) _____
I am praying to you.

Thank you, ___(name of person you want to forgive or be forgiven by)___
for doing to me all that you have done.

Forgive me, ___(name of person you want to forgive or be forgiven by)___
for all that I have done to you.

_____ (Your own name) _____ *, I am praying to you.*

Thank you, _____ (your own name) _____
for doing to me all that you have done.

Forgive me, _____ (your own name) _____ *,*
for all that I have done to you.

The Prayer to Free You of Resentment

Beloved Savior, _____ (name of person you hate) _____

is Thine as I am Thine. Make it right between us. Amen

Bibliography

Byrne, Rhonda. *The Secret* New York: Atria Books/ Beyond Words, 2006.

Cayce, Edgar. Edgar Cayce Readings. Virginia Beach, VA: Edgar Cayce Foundation, 1971, 1993-2010.

Chapman, Carol. *Arrival of the Gods in Egypt: Hidden Mysteries of Soul and Myth Finally Revealed.* Foster, VA: SunTopaz, 2008.

Chapman, Carole. *When We Were Gods: Insights on Atlantis, Past Lives, Angelic Beings of Light, and Spiritual Awakening.* Foster, VA: SunTopaz, 2005.

Chapman, Carole A.P. *The Golden Ones: From Atlantis to a New World.* Mystic, Ct: CPS, 2001.

Christie, Agatha. *The Body in the Library.* New York: Pocket Books, 1955.

_____. *Nemesis.* New York: Pocket Books, 1972.

_____. *A Pocket Full of Rye.* New York: Pocket Books, 1954.

_____. *Sleeping Murder.* Dodd, Meade & Co., 1976.

Churchill, Winston. (n.d.). Quotation Details: Quotation #3257 from Laura Moncur's Motivational Quotations. The Quotations Page. Retrieved November 19, 2010, from www.quotationspage.com/quote/3257.html.

Dickinson, Emily. Quotations by Author: Emily Dickenson (1830-1886). The Quotations Page. Retrieved November

19, 2010, from www.quotationspage.com/quotes/ Emily_ Dickinson.

Einstein, Albert. *Bite-Size Einstein: Quotations on Just About Everything from the Greatest Mind of the Twentieth Century.* Compiled by Jerry Mayer and John P. Holms. New York: St. Martin's Press, 1996.

Irion, J. Everett. "The 40-Day Prayer." *Venture Inward* September/October 1985: 8-9.

———. *Why Do We Dream?* Virginia Beach, VA: A.R.E. Press, 1990.

Joseph, Arthur Samuel. *Vocal Power: Harnessing the Power Within.* Encino, California: Vocal Awareness Institute, 2003.

Lincoln, Abraham. "I have been driven many times ..." *QuoteWorld.* Retrieved November 27, 2010, from http://quoteworld.org/quotes/10275.

Metzger, Bruce M. and Roland E. Murphy, eds. *The Revised Standard Version of the Bible: The New Oxford Annotated Bible with Apocrypha.* New York: Oxford University Press, 1991.

Mother Teresa. The most poignant quotes: Forgiveness. Poignant Quotes. Retrieved November 19, 2010, from www.stevenredhead.com/quotes/poignant/Forgiven ess.html.

"Overcoming Hatred with Love." *Friends of Peace Pilgrim: A newsletter dedicated to spreading Peace Pilgrim's message of overcoming evil with good, falsehood with truth & hatred with love.* Number 1. Harvest time, 1987. Retrieved 2005, from www.peacepilgrim.com/FoPP/newsletter/ nl01.htm#OVERCOMING.

Proctor, Bob. *You Were Born Rich: Now You Can Discover and Develop Those Riches.* Scottsdale, Arizona: LifeSuccess Productions, 1997.

The Secret. DVD. Dir. Drew Heriot. With Rhonda Byrne, Jack Canfield, Bob Proctor, Denis Waitley, Neale Donald Walsh. TS Production, LLC., 2006. 92 minutes.

Stormwolf, Alison and Pat Wilson. Native American Wisdom, Philosophy, Quotes. An Indian Story. (Lakota Sioux Chief Yellow Lark, Trans. 1887). Soul-Awakening. Retrieved November 19, 2010, from www.soul-awakening.com/philosophy/native-american-wisdom.htm.

Synchronicity. Wikipedia. Retrieved November 19, 2010, from http://en.wikipedia.org/wiki/Synchronicity.

Twain, Mark. "Letter to the Earth." *Letters from the Earth.* Ed. Bernard Devoto. Fawcett Books, 1962.

Tzu, Lao. Lao Tzu Quotes. Brainy Quote. Retrieved November 19, 2010, from www.brainyquote.com/quotes/quotes/l/laotzu169451.html.

_____. Lao Tzu Quotes. ThinkExist.com. Retrieved November 19, 2010 from http://thinkexist.com/quotation/health_is_the_greatest_possession-contentment_is/213950.html.

Wattles, Wallace D. *The Science of Getting Rich: A Lawful Process for the Creation of Wealth.* Scottsdale, Arizona: LifeSuccess Productions, 1996.

Webster's Dictionary: New Revised and Expanded Edition. Ashland, Ohio: Landoll, 1993.

Microsoft Word. 2003. Thesaurus developed by Bloomsbury Publishing Plc. Microsoft Corporation, 1983-2002.

Princeton University. WordNet. Retrieved 2007, from http://wordnet.princeton.edu/perl/webwn?.

Index

Acknowledgements

I feel so happy and grateful to have known J. Everett Irion and to have had the blessings of his advice and teachings. In addition, Edgar Cayce's psychic readings have been a wonderful help in my life from learning how to receive guidance in my dreams, to information that led to better health, to wisdom showing me how to connect with my purpose in life. I also appreciate the wonderful community developed by Edgar Cayce's Association for Research and Enlightenment (A.R.E.), which provides books and multi-media products describing Cayce's trance readings. The A.R.E. is headquartered in Virginia Beach, Virginia, with outreach throughout the world—I first heard about Edgar Cayce when I lived in Toronto, Canada.

In addition, I appreciate Nancy C. Chrisbaum's informative and entertaining Foreword that further brought J. Everett Irion alive for the reader. I am also grateful for conversations about Everett I had with Susan Lendvay, editor-in-chief of Edgar Cayce's membership magazine, *Venture Inward*. And, I really appreciate the fine work and support from Claire Gardner at the Edgar Cayce Foundation in reviewing all quotes taken from the Edgar Cayce readings and making sure they are accurate.

My proofreaders are wonderful. Thank you, Lindy van Burik, Cynthia Hastings, Cathy Hunsberger, and Una Marcotte for all your help.

Finally, I am deeply grateful for Clair Balsley, my editor at SunTopaz, who took the raw material of my manuscript and polished it until it shone. She designed the book, including the cover, and is the webmaster that created my marvelous website.

Other Books by the Author

When We Were Gods
Insights on Atlantis, Past Lives, Angelic Beings of Light, and Spiritual Awakening
ISBN: 978-0-9754691-1-8

When We Were Gods is the remarkable true story of a spiritual awakening. When an ordinary woman goes to a hypnotherapist for weight control, she not only finds past life reasons for her problem, but she also connects with former realms and the fabulous world of Atlantis. She travels to Yucatan, Mexico and finds confirmation of her Atlantean memories in the ruins of the ancient Maya.

Powerful spiritual guides also appear in her hypnosis sessions with messages for her to convey to humanity. They reveal the reason for our present trials and offer hope for the future.

When We Were Gods: Insights on Atlantis, Past Lives, Angelic Beings of Light, and Spiritual Awakening is the revised, updated edition of *The Golden Ones: From Atlantis to a New World.*

Find out more at
www.CarolEChapman.com/books.html

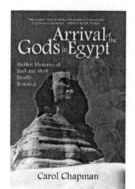

Arrival of the Gods in Egypt
Hidden Mysteries of Soul and
Myth Finally Revealed
ISBN: 978-0-9754691-5-6

During past-life regression, Carol sees herself falling into the mouth of a snake to be transported from a sinking Atlantis to Egypt during the time when the pyramids were built. Intrigued with her past-life hypnosis, she decides to visit Egypt to discover the meaning of her past-life memories.

In addition to decoding this and other mysteries from Egyptian tomb paintings, Carol learns of the recent apparitions of the Blessed Virgin Mary in Egypt that are taking place in a city barred from tourists. *Arrival of the Gods in Egypt* holds amazing adventures full of intriguing discoveries about mysteries both past and present.

In this fascinating book you will learn about Edgar Cayce's psychic readings on the gods of Egypt. You will also unearth connections between the ancient Maya and the Egyptians.

Arrival of the Gods in Egypt: Hidden Mysteries of Soul and Myth Finally Revealed is the follow up to *When We Were Gods* (which is the revised edition of *The Golden Ones*).

Find out more at
www.CarolEChapman.com/books.html

Other SunTopaz Items

BOOK
Tales from the Yucatan Jungle
Life in a Mayan Village
by Kristine Ellingson
ISBN: 978-0-9754691-8-7

Where would you go if you needed to get away from it all? What would happen if you never came back? Your life would change forever as it did for Kristine Ellingson. She left her home in the U.S. and moved to the vibrant land of the ancient Maya.

Kristine Ellingson was a successful American jewelry designer with two grown children and a marriage on the rocks. She left her home in Oregon for a trip to Yucatan, Mexico that she believed would be an extended vacation. Much to her surprise, her stop in Yucatan was permanent.

Join Kristine as she recounts her journey in finding a new home and family in a peaceful village near the Mayan ruins of Uxmal. In spite of being an outsider and looking nothing like the Mayas—she is tall and blonde—she is accepted by the village and becomes an integral part of their community. Kristine allows readers to glimpse a world seldom seen by outsiders.

Find out more at www.SunTopaz.com/books.html

DVD
Yucatan Travel
Cancun to Chichen Itza
by Carol Chapman
Narrated by Miriam Balsley
UPC: 8 52049 00300 5

Do you wonder what to expect when you visit Mayan ruins, Caribbean beaches, and Mexican Colonial cities? Are you curious about traveling among the peaceful Maya? Join Yucatan traveler Miriam Balsley as she explores Cancun, Coba, Tulum, Chichen Itza, Valladolid, Izamal, Ek Balam, Cozumel, Akumal, and Playa del Carmen.

If you're wondering what to expect if you venture out of Cancun on an excursion and feel afraid to take the risk in a foreign country that speaks mainly Spanish, this DVD will calm your fears as it follows typical tourists—a husband, wife, and their grown daughter—as they enjoy the genuine Mayan food, relax in a hammock beside the pool of their hotel, explore archeological wonders, swim in the warm aquamarine waters of the Caribbean Sea, and talk with Mayan people in the wonderful, beautiful land of Yucatan.

Find out more at www.Suntopaz.com

About the Author

Photo by David A. Seaver

Carol Chapman is an internationally acclaimed author, lecturer, and filmmaker. A keynote speaker at weekend spiritual retreats, her seminars are not only informative and transformational but also fun and entertaining. She also enjoys sharing her information through online media, book signings, and radio interviews.

Chapman has appeared in person as a speaker and workshop leader in many places including New York, Texas, Virginia, and Alaska in the U.S.A, and Nova Scotia, Ontario, and British Columbia in Canada. Some of her radio appearances include the Maria Shaw Show and Coast-to-Coast AM (Art Bell and George Noory).

Chapman's other books include *Arrival of the Gods in Egypt* and *When We Were God*, which is the revised, updated version of *The Golden Ones*. She has also had many articles published in magazines such as *Venture Inward, FATE, Dream Network, Alternate Perceptions,* and *Whole Life Times.*

As a filmmaker, Chapman created the family travel documentary *Yucatan Travel: Cancun to Chichen Itza.* She is also an award-winning photographer and while working under contract to N.A.S.A., her photos appeared in publications throughout the world including *Air and Space Smithsonian, Aeronautique Astronautique* (France), *Aeronautica & Difesa* (Italy), *Details,* and *Aerospace America.*

Occasionally her first name has been spelled with an "e' on the end, resulting in some of her works being listed as by "Carole Chapman" while others are listed as by "Carol Chapman." Her preference is for Carol (without the "e").

Chapman obtained a Bachelor's degree in Journalism from Prescott College in Arizona, U.S.A. and also studied Photography and Filmmaking at Ryerson University in Toronto, Canada.

Chapman and her husband love to travel. They live on a river in southeastern Virginia where they enjoy sailing.

Contact Information for Carol Chapman

Web Site: www.CarolEChapman.com

Blog: www.CarolChapmanLive.com

Email: CarolChapman@SunTopaz.com

Carol Chapman can also be found on Facebook.

CPSIA information can be obtained at www.ICGtesting.com
Printed in the USA
LVOW08s0554031013

355217LV00001B/6/P